Chameleons

And Other Animals
With Amazing Skin

by

Susan Labella

Children's Press®
A Division of Scholastic Inc.
New York   Toronto   London   Auckland   Sydney
Mexico City   New Delhi   Hong Kong
Danbury, Connecticut

These content vocabulary word
builders are for grades 1 -2.

Consultant: Edward I. Pollak, Ph.D.
Biopsychologist and Herpetoculturist
Department of Psychology
West Chester University of Pennsylvania

Reading Specialist: Don Curry

Special thanks to Omaha's Henry Doorly Zoo

Photo Credits:

Photographs © 2005: Corbis Images: 23 bottom right (Reinhard Eisele), cover right inset, 5 bottom, 19 top, 19 bottom (Stephen Frink), 20 bottom (David A. Northcott), 23 top right (Royalty-Free), 4 bottom left, 5 top left, 14, 15 bottom (Kennan Ward), 20 top (Stuart Westmorland); Dembinsky Photo Assoc.: cover background (E. R. Degginger), 2, 4 bottom right, 17 (A. B. Sheldon); Dwight R. Kuhn Photography: 11, 13; National Geographic Image Collection: 7 (Chis Johns), cover left inset (Paul Nicklen), 4 top, 15 top (Norbert Rosing); Nature Picture Library Ltd./Ingo Arndt: back cover, 21 bottom; NHPA: 1 (James Carmichael Jr.), 21 top (Nick Garbutt), 5 top right, 9; Photo Researchers, NY: 23 top left (Nick Bergkessel Jr.), cover center inset (Dr. Paul A. Zahl); Stock Boston/Bob Daemmrich: 23 bottom left.

Book Design: Simonsays Design!

Library of Congress Cataloging-in-Publication Data
Labella, Susan, 1948-
    Chameleons and other animals with amazing skin / by Susan Labella.
        p. cm. — (Scholastic news nonfiction readers)
    Includes bibliographical references and index.
    ISBN 0-516-24925-8 (lib. bdg.)
    1. Skin—Juvenile literature. 2. Chameleons—Juvenile literature. I. Title.
        II. Series.
    QL941.L33 2005
    573.5—dc22

                                                                        2005003096

1 2 3 4 5 6 7 8 9 10 R 14 13 12 11 10 09 08 07 06 05

CONTENTS

Word Hunt 4-5

Skin! Skin! 6-7

A Chameleon's Skin 8-9

Chameleons Get Mad 10-11

More About a Chameleon's Skin . . 12-13

Arctic Hare Skin 14-15

Poison Arrow Frog 16-17

Puffer Fish Skin 18-19

Chameleons Change Color! 20-21

Your New Words 22

These Animals Have Amazing

    Skin, Too! 23

Index 24

Find Out More 24

Meet the Author 24

WORD HUNT

Look for these words as you read. They will be in **bold**.

arctic hare
(**ark**-tik hair)

fur
(fur)

poisonous skir
(**poi**-zuhn-us skir

4

camouflage
(**kam**-uh-flahzh)

chameleon
(kuh-**mee**-lee-uhn)

puffer fish
(**puh**-fir fish)

stretch
(strech)

5

Skin! Skin!

How do animals use their skin?

Some animals use their skin to help them hide.

Other animals have skin that tastes bad.

Their skin can hurt other animals.

Let's look at some animals that have amazing skin!

Can you see the chameleon?
It has skin that helps it hide.

A **chameleon's** skin changes colors.

First it's green, like a leaf.

Then it's brown, like a branch.

The colors of a chameleon's skin help it hide from predators.

A predator is an animal that will eat the chameleon.

This African chameleon is green, like the leaves around it.

Some chameleons turn red and yellow when they are mad.

Other chameleons turn blue or pink.

These chameleons get dark spots on their skin.

Look how their skin changes.
Now they have spots on their skin.

A chameleon's skin can show if it is hot or cold, too.

If it is cold, its skin gets dark to take in heat.

If it is warm, its skin becomes a lighter color.

his chameleon is cold. So, its skin
gets dark. A leaf covers its cold body.

ook! The leaf kept it warm.
Now its skin color is lighter.

13

An **arctic hare** changes colors, too.

Its **fur** changes from brown in spring, to white in winter.

These colors **camouflage**, or hide, the hare from predators.

camouflage

Winter is coming. This hare's fur
changing from brown to white.

ook! Now its fur is
white like the snow.

15

Don't eat this animal!

A poison arrow frog has **poisonous skin**.

The poison kills animals that eat it.

The poison arrow frog
is very colorful.

Don't let this fish fool you!

The **puffer fish** has amazing skin, too.

It sucks in air or water when an enemy is near.

Its skin **stretches** out to make the fish look bigger.

This scares the enemy off.

Watch this puffer fish get bigger!

Now it has points on it. Ouch!

CHAMELEON

This is a Panther chameleon. Its skin changes color to warn other chameleons to stay away.

1

Look! Its skin is red now. There must be another chameleon close by.

2

CHANGE COLOR!

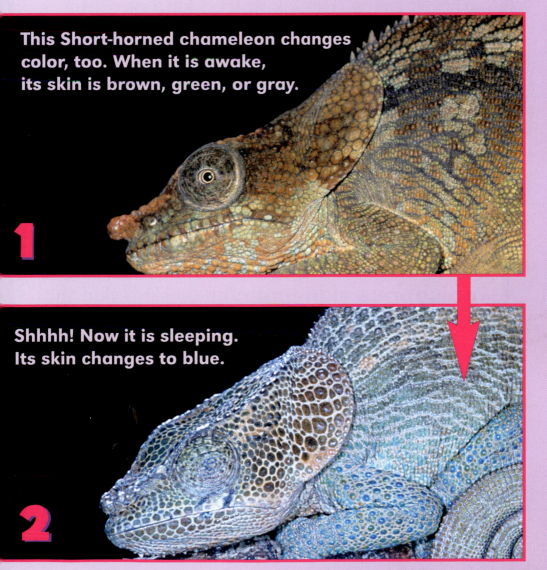

1 This Short-horned chameleon changes color, too. When it is awake, its skin is brown, green, or gray.

2 Shhhh! Now it is sleeping. Its skin changes to blue.

YOUR NEW WORDS

arctic hare (**ark**-tik hair) a kind of rabbit that lives near the north pole

camouflage (**kam**-uh-flahzh) a color or covering that helps an animal hide

chameleon (kuh-**mee**-lee-uhn) a kind of lizard

fur (fur) the hairy coat of an animal

poisonous skin (**poi**-zuhn-us skin) skin that can hurt or kill an animal that eats it

puffer fish (**puh**-fir fish) a kind of fish that has skin that stretches

stretch (strech) to make something bigger or change its shape

THESE ANIMALS HAVE AMAZING SKIN, TOO!

flying squirrel

frill-necked lizard

human

rhinocerous

INDEX

arctic hare, 4, 14

camouflage, 5, 14
chameleons, 5, 8, 10, 12
colors, 8, 12, 14

fish, 5, 18
frogs, 16
fur, 4, 14

poison arrow frogs, 16
poisonous skin, 4, 16

predators, 8, 14
puffer fish, 5, 18

spots, 10
stretching, 5, 18

FIND OUT MORE

Book:
Whose Skin Is This?: A Look at Animal Skin—Scaly, Furry, and Prickly
by Lisa Morris Kee and Ken Landmark

Website:
http://www.enchantedlearning.com/coloring/w.shtml

MEET THE AUTHOR:

Susan Labella is a writer of books, articles, and magazines for kids. She is the author of other books in the Scholastic News Nonfiction Readers series. She lives in rural Connecticut where she sees turtles and birds.